Ge

OVERCOMING FEAR, HANDLING STRESS, HANDLING CRITICISM & REJECTION, HANDLING RUDE PEOPLE, HANDLING TOUGH SITUATIONS & GETTING RID OF BAD HABITS!

Written By Joy Berry
Illustrated by Bartholomew

Copyright © 2008 by Joy Berry
All rights reserved. Published by Joy Berry Enterprises, 146 West 29th St.,
Suite 11RW, New York, NY 10001

No part of this publication may be reproduced in whole or in part, or
stored in a retrieval system, or transmitted in any form or by any means,
electronic, mechanical, photocopying, recording, or otherwise, without
written permission of the author. For information regarding permission
write to Joy Berry,

Joy Berry Enterprises
146 West 29th St., Suite 11RW
New York, NY 10001

Cover Design & Art Direction: John Bellaud
Art Production: Geoff Glisson

ISBN 978-1-60577-603-3

You Can...
Get Over It!

Table of Contents

SELF-TALK MESSAGES
IN GET OVER IT!

• THE POWER OF YOUR MIND

Your mind is extremely powerful. In fact, your thoughts affect everything that you do. If you think positive thoughts, you will most likely act in positive ways and bring positive things into your life. Conversely, if you think negative thoughts, you will most likely act in negative ways and bring negative things into your life.

• SELF - TALK

Self-talk is a way of communicating positive or negative thoughts to yourself. The most common forms of self-talk include thinking, talking, and writing to yourself.

THINKING TO YOURSELF	TALKING TO YOURSELF	WRITING TO YOURSELF
Negative Thinking: "There is no way that I can win this competition. I wish it was over."	Negative Talking: "There is no way that I am going to do well on the test. I am not prepared."	Negative Writing: "Dear Diary, Nothing has ever gone right for me and nothing is ever going to change."
Positive Thinking: "I am going to give my best effort to this competition because I want to win."	Positive Talking: "I am well prepared and will do well on the test. I feel confident."	Positive Writing: "Dear Diary, Although I am going through tough times, I can make things better."

• MESSAGES IN GET OVER IT!

This book includes positive self-talk messages that can help you do the following:

OVERCOME FEAR - HANDLE STRESS - HANDLE CRITICISM & REJECTION
HANDLE RUDE PEOPLE - HANDLE TOUGH SITUATIONS - GET RID OF BAD HABITS

There are eight self-talk messages at the end of each of the six sections in this book. By memorizing these messages and repeating them to yourself over and over again, you will begin to integrate the statements into the way that you perceive yourself and your world. And, as you do this, you will begin to think, and then act, in more positive ways. In the end, this will make you a happier, more successful person.

Get Over It!

Overcome Fear

You can overcome fear if you
- understand what fear is,
- know what causes fear,
- recognize the differences between healthy and unhealthy fears, and
- follow the six steps for dealing with your fears.

Fear is a strong, unpleasant feeling.

LET'S CLIMB UP THIS TREE AND GET A BETTER LOOK AT THE VIEW.

NO THANKS, I CAN SEE ENOUGH OF THE VIEW FROM THE GROUND.

You might feel afraid when you become aware of danger or when you expect something bad to happen.

Fear can cause you to panic. You might feel out of control and want to run away.

Fear can cause you to hate something and not want to be around it.

UGH!

IT'S FOR YOUR OWN GOOD!

BUT I'M SCARED OF HEIGHTS!

Fear might cause your body to react in ways that cause you to feel uncomfortable.

■ Your heart might beat faster.
■ You might breathe harder.
■ You might begin to perspire.

■ Your stomach might feel upset.
■ Your muscles might feel tense.
■ You might feel weak.

AMAZING! HIS FACE IS CHANGING COLORS FASTER THAN THE LEAVES!

When you were a baby, you probably were less fearful than you are now because there were people in your life who protected you and took care of you.

When you were a baby, you were kept safe in your crib, your playpen, your high chair, or your parent's arms.

WARDEN, I'M INNOCENT, I TELL YA. I'M INNOCENT!

As you grew and began to explore the world around you, you learned that you could get hurt.

AH-HA! SO THAT FLAME IS **HOT!** I NEED TO REMEMBER THAT WHEN I START COOKING!

You learned to be afraid of certain things.

Firsthand experiences have taught you to be afraid of certain things.

WHY DON'T YOU LIKE TO CLIMB TREES?

I STILL CAN'T FIGURE OUT WHAT SPECIES HE BELONGS TO.

BIRDS of a Feather

Whenever you experienced something that hurt you, you learned to be afraid of it.

THE LAST TIME I CLIMBED A TREE, I FELL AND BROKE MY LEG!

IS IT OVER?

Secondhand experiences taught you to be afraid of certain things.

■ You might have observed someone getting hurt and learned to fear whatever caused that person to get hurt.

■ You might have heard about something that could harm you, and you learned to fear it.

FRANKLIN WAS EATING CHOCOLATE CAKE, STUFFING HIS FACE AS USUAL, WHEN HE BEGAN TO CHOKE...

WOW! I'LL NEVER EAT CHOCOLATE CAKE AGAIN!

THAT HAPPENED TO ME ONCE, WHEN I WAS EATING A HOT DOG!

■ You might have learned to be afraid through experiencing the fears of others.

Sometimes you became afraid because other people were afraid.

IF MOM'S AFRAID OF THE DARK, IT **MUST** BE DANGEROUS!

HMMMM...

SNiFF SNiFF

You became afraid because of something you felt other people were thinking and feeling.

Some of your fears are **healthy.** Healthy fears are appropriate responses to what you are afraid of.

Healthy fears are the result of wise, intelligent thinking.

Healthy fears are usually good for you. They warn you of dangerous situations.

Healthy fears might help you avoid doing something dangerous. They might keep you from hurting yourself or others.

HONK

NOW YOU KNOW WHY I'M AFRAID TO JAYWALK!

SCREEECH

Some of your fears might be **unhealthy.**
Unhealthy fears are inappropriate responses to
what you are afraid of.

Unhealthy fears are either **exaggerated,
irrational,** or **displaced.**

An *exaggerated* fear makes something seem
worse than it actually is.

ACTUALLY, I **DON'T** CARE IF
I GO. IT'S GOING TO BE
HORRIBLE! I WON'T KNOW ANYONE.
I WON'T KNOW WHAT TO DO.
I'LL LOOK LIKE AN IDIOT.

An *irrational* fear is one that does not make any sense.

HEY, YOU GEEK!

THEY WON'T LIKE ME! THEY'LL MAKE FUN OF ME. THEY'LL BEAT ME UP! THEY'LL TEAR MY HEAD OFF!

AND I THOUGHT THE KENNEL WAS BAD.

A *displaced* fear is a made-up fear that takes the place of a real one.

Exaggerated, irrational, and displaced fears are not good for you. They can cause you to feel out of control. They can cause you to do something that you do not want to do.

Unhealthy fears can also prevent you from doing the things that you need or want to do.

I CAN'T GO! I WON'T GO! THEY'LL NEVER TAKE ME ALIVE! NO WAY!

BUT YOU NEED TO GO TO SCHOOL!

I KNOW A GREAT CANINE TRAINING CLASS HE COULD ATTEND.

Whether your fears are healthy or unhealthy, you must pay attention to them. You must also learn to handle them appropriately if you are going to live a happy, productive life.

Pretending that you are not afraid when you actually are afraid is not a good way to handle your fears.

OOOH...AHH...WHO? ME? HEH HEH. IS THERE SCHOOL TODAY? I UM...AHHH...GUESS I FORGOT. UM, NO PROBLEM. I'LL GO TOMORROW.

HEH HEH.

YEAH, RIGHT. AND I LIKE CATS!

Sometimes you might want to ask someone to help you work on handling your fears. Make sure that the person you ask is wise enough to give you the assistance that you need.

Whether you work with someone or work alone, there are things that you can do to help yourself deal with your fears.

Step 1: Face it. Admit to yourself that you are afraid.

Step 2: Accept it. Remember that everyone experiences fear. Therefore, you need not be embarrassed about feeling afraid.

Step 3: Think about it. Ask yourself, "Can the thing I'm afraid of actually hurt me?"

CAN THE THING I'M AFRAID OF REALLY HURT ME?

HMMM..

ONLY IF IT HAS LOTS OF SHARP TEETH AND FUR!

Step 4: Understand it. Realize that when you don't know the truth about something, you often make up your own ideas about it. The ideas that you make up can be terrifying, even if they are not true. Therefore, understanding something that you are afraid of can help you to overcome your fear of it.

To understand what you are afraid of, you need to learn as much as possible about it.

Research can help you to accomplish this.

You can do research by observing, exploring, experimenting, reading, and viewing educational programs on computers and TV.

Continue to do your research until you understand what you are afraid of.

Step 5: Decide what to do about it. Eliminate, escape, or confront what is causing your fear.

Eliminating what is causing your fear

Sometimes the easiest way to deal with your fear is to get rid of what is causing it.

Getting rid of what is causing your fear will work in some situations. However, it will not work in every situation.

KA-RACKLE KA-BOOM

HOW DO YOU GET RID OF A THUNDER STORM?

EAR PLUGS?!

Escaping what is causing your fear

Sometimes you can avoid or run away from the thing that is causing you to be afraid.

THOSE GUYS **REALLY** SCARE ME. I'M GLAD I DON'T HAVE ANY CLASSES WITH THEM.

Escaping what is causing your fear will work in some situations. However, it will not work in every situation.

THIS YEAR, WE DECIDED TO PUT ALL THE GRADES TOGETHER FOR GYM. SO YOU'LL ALL BE TOGETHER THIS PERIOD.

GULP!

Confronting what is causing your fear

Sometimes you need to face and do something about what is causing your fear.

Confronting what is causing your fear will work in some situations. However, it will not work in every situation.

I STOOD UP TO THOSE OLDER GUYS AND IT WORKED. I WONDER IF IT COULD WORK IN THIS SITUATION?

NICE DOGGIE!

GGRRRRR

I DON'T THINK SO. I KNOW THIS GUY!

Step 6: Do what you have decided to do.

Follow through on your plan to eliminate, escape, or confront what is causing your fear.

BUT I THINK THIS TIME IT WOULD BE BETTER TO ESCAPE WHAT'S CAUSING MY FEAR.

BARK BARK BARK HELP!

You might need to complete Step 6 gradually. This means that you do it slowly, over a period of time.

Or you might need to do Step 6 "cold." This means you do it quickly, all at once.

FIRST I'LL TRY TO GET CLOSE ENOUGH TO TALK TO HIM. THEN I'LL TRY FEEDING HIM, THEN MAYBE...

Here are some things that people commonly fear:

- animals
- being alone
- changes
- dying
- falling

- getting hurt
- ghosts
- high places
- failing
- rejection

- natural disasters
- performing
- criticism
- large things
- losing someone
- loud noises
- speaking in public
- strangers
- the dark
- thunderstorms
- unfamiliar places
- water

Fears seldom go away on their own. If you do not process them properly when you are younger, you might still have them when you become older. This might keep you from living a healthy, productive life.

Therefore, if you have a fear, no matter how small you think it is, you must deal with it. Doing this will help you to grow and to become a better person.

Overcome Fear
AFFIRMATIONS

- My fear originates in my mind.

- I am in control of my mind.

- I will not allow my fear to control me.

- I will control my fear.

Overcome Fear
AFFIRMATIONS

- I will pay attention to my fear.

- I will respond to whatever my fear is telling me.

- I will work to eliminate, escape or control my fear.

- I will overcome my fear.

Get Over It!

Handle Stress

You can handle stress if you
- know what causes stress,
- understand how stress affects you,
- learn the four ways to deal with stress, and
- prepare yourself to deal with stress.

Stress is your reaction to unsettling situations. It is the way you feel and act when something disturbing happens.

An upsetting situation that causes stress is called a **stressor**. A stressor is anything that is overly unsettling.

...YOUR REPORT WILL REPRESENT ONE-QUARTER OF YOUR FINAL GRADE...

UMPHHH...

THUMP

I'D SAY THIS QUALIFIES AS A FULL-FLEDGED STRESSOR.

Some stressors are positive. **Positive stressors** cause you to feel good or to benefit in some way.

Some stressors are negative. **Negative stressors** cause unpleasant feelings and stress that can harm you.

I'VE GOT TO CLEAN MY ROOM, TAKE OUT THE TRASH, AND WASH THE CAR. THEN I'VE GOT TO HELP WITH THE SCHOOL PLAY AND DO THIS HOMEWORK. HOW CAN I DO IT ALL? I'M ONLY ONE PERSON...

BY THE WAY, I NEED MY LITTER BOX CHANGED.

Four kinds of negative stressors can cause stress:

1. Negative Stressors Involving Your Body

Injury can cause stress.

Illness can cause stress.

2. Negative Stressors Involving Others

Conflict is disagreeing with someone. When you have a conflict with someone, you might have difficulty getting along with that person. You even might argue with him or her. Conflict can cause stress.

Rejection is a feeling of being unwanted. It is the feeling that you are not liked or not accepted by others. Rejection can cause stress.

GO FIND ANOTHER GAME!

NO ONE EVER WANTS ME TO PLAY ON THEIR TEAM.

SIGH

YOUR PROBLEM IS NOTHING THAT BEING THREE FEET TALLER WOULDN'T CURE!

Loss is what you feel when you lose something that is important to you. It is also what you experience when someone you care about
■ dies,
■ moves away from you, or
■ leaves you and does not return.
Loss can cause stress.

OH, NO! I'VE LOST MY REPORT!

HE'S LOST HIS COOL!

3. Negative Stressors Involving Your Behavior

Misbehavior is doing something that you know is wrong. When you misbehave, you might feel guilty or afraid of getting into trouble. Misbehavior can cause stress.

An *unfamiliar experience* is doing something that you have never done before or have not done very often. Unfamiliar experiences can cause stress.

BUT I'VE NEVER DONE THIS BEFORE! I WON'T KNOW ANYONE. I CAN'T EVEN DANCE!

BELIEVE ME, YOU'LL HAVE A GREAT TIME.

AcCKK...

I DIDN'T KNOW DANCING COULD BE A STRESSOR!

Failure is not succeeding at something that you try to do. Failure can cause stress.

4. Negative Stressors Involving Your Surroundings

Uncontrollable events are events that you cannot control. Having your parents divorce and having to move are examples of uncontrollable events that can cause stress.

Unpredictable events are events that can happen without your knowing when they will begin or end. Unexpected accidents and natural disasters such as earthquakes and tornadoes are unpredictable events that can cause stress.

Other negative stressors involving your surroundings include
- irritating noises,
- extreme heat,
- extreme cold, and
- large crowds.

Here are some common stressors that young people often experience:

- Death of a family member or friend
- Death of a pet
- Having parents divorce or remarry
- Getting into trouble at home or at school
- Attending a new school
- Getting injured
- Getting sick
- Fighting with family members or friends
- Not having enough money to buy the things that are wanted or needed
- Moving to a new location
- Taking a test
- Struggling to get good grades
- Participating in an "important" competition
- Losing something that is important
- Peer pressure

Most people react *physically* when they
experience a stressor. Your body might react
in one or more of these ways:

- You might breathe faster.
- Your blood pressure might increase.
- You might break out in a "cold sweat."
- Your face might turn pale.
- Your muscles might tense up.
- You might feel nauseous.

Your body's reactions to a negative stressor are
called *physical stress.*

Most people also react **emotionally** when they experience a stressor. If you experience a negative stressor, you most likely will have one or more of these feelings:

■ Anxiety
■ Frustration
■ A feeling of helplessness or being out of control
■ Resentment
■ Depression
■ Anger

Your emotional reactions to a negative stressor are called **emotional stress.**

Your chances of suffering a great deal of physical and emotional stress are greater when you
■ experience many stressors at the same time or
■ experience one stressor over a very long time.

TOO MUCH PHYSICAL AND EMOTIONAL STRESS IS NOT GOOD FOR YOU.

OH, MAN. THIS GUY'S BRILLIANT.

SIGH!

Too much physical and emotional stress can cause you to have physical problems, such as stomachaches, headaches, or backaches. Physical and emotional stress can also cause you to become sick.

Too much physical and emotional stress can make you unhappy.

I CAN'T REMEMBER THE LAST TIME I FELT HAPPY!

OH SURE...IT WAS WHEN YOU BROUGHT YOUR CUTE LITTLE KITTY HOME.

Stress can make you feel cranky and can cause you to be unfair or unkind to the people around you. This could harm your relationships with others.

Too much physical and emotional stress can be distracting. It can keep you from thinking clearly, and it can make learning difficult.

Stress can also keep you from doing what
needs to be done.

IT'S **IMPOSSIBLE** TO DO MY SCHOOL WORK WITH EVERYTHING ELSE I HAVE ON MY MIND... HOW AM I EVER GOING TO **FINISH?**

DON'T CALL ON ME... PLEASE DON'T CALL ON ME... PLEASE, OH PLEASE...

Too much physical and emotional stress can lead to the development of bad habits, such as biting your nails or eating too much.

Stress can keep you from falling asleep or
sleeping soundly. It can also cause you to have
nightmares, be restless, or grind your teeth
while you are sleeping.

TOSS TURN

NOW I CAN'T
SLEEP. I'M OUT
OF HERE!

You can learn to deal with physical and emotional stress. Depending upon the circumstances, you can
- avoid negative stressors,
- overcome negative stressors,
- adjust to negative stressors, or
- relieve the stress caused by negative stressors.

1. Avoiding Negative Stressors

If possible, avoid being around people, places, and situations that upset you. Also, try not to do things that upset you.

2. Overcoming Negative Stressors

If you can not avoid a negative stressor, you might need to overcome it. Solve the problems that negative stressors cause by following these steps:

Step One: Decide what problem needs to be solved.

Step Two: Decide what the possible solutions are.

Step Three: Consider the advantages and disadvantages that each solution offers.

ONE OF MY BIGGEST PROBLEMS IS MY SCIENCE GRADES...

WHATEVER IS GROWING UNDER THIS BED WOULD MAKE A GREAT SCIENCE PROJECT!

Step Four: Choose the best solution.

Step Five: Do what needs to be done to solve the problem.

Step Six: Think about whether or not your actions have solved the problem in the best possible way.

3. Adjusting to Negative Stressors

If circumstances make it impossible to avoid or to overcome a negative stressor, you might need to accept it. Realize that it is part of your life. Learn to live with it.

4. Relieving the Stress Caused by Negative Stressors

You can help to relieve stress in one or more of the following ways:

- Positive self-talk
- Positive thinking
- Relaxation
- Exercise
- Emotional support
- Communication

GETTING UP HERE WAS EASY. NOW, HOW DO I GET DOWN?

Positive self-talk is giving yourself messages that will help you feel calm and reassured. Here are some examples of positive self-talk messages to use when you experience stress:

■ "I have handled problems in the past, so I know I can also handle this."
■ "Things have always worked out in the past, so I know that this will work out, also."
■ "Like every other problem, this problem has a solution."
■ "Something good always comes out of difficult experiences. So, I know something good will come out of this experience."
■ "Things are usually not as bad as they seem. So, this situation is not as bad as it seems."
■ "There's a good reason for everything that happens. So I know that there is a good reason why this is happening."

Positive thinking involves clearing your mind of negative thoughts by replacing them with positive thoughts. When you need some positive thoughts to replace negative ones, think about

- a past experience that you have enjoyed,
- a future event that you are going to enjoy,
- being in a place that you truly enjoy,
- doing something that you truly enjoy,
- becoming the kind of person that you want to become, or
- being with someone you like.

NO DOUBT HE'S RECALLING THE DAY HE BROUGHT ME HOME. I WAS SO CUTE AND CUDDLY.

Relaxation is slowing down your mind and body and encouraging them to rest.

Here is one way to relax your body: First, find a quiet place where you will not be disturbed. Lie flat on your back, stretch your legs out, place your feet slightly apart, put your arms close to your sides, turn the palms of your hands up, and close your eyes.

While you are in this position, silently count to ten. With each count, tense a part of your body, beginning with your head. By the time you reach ten, your body should be completely tense from head to toe.

After you have completely tensed your body, begin again to count to ten. With each count, relax a part of your body, beginning with your toes.

Think to yourself, "My toes are completely relaxed." As you think this, relax your toes. Next, think to yourself, "My feet are completely relaxed," and relax your feet. Do the same with your legs. Then do the same thing with every other part of your body. By the time you reach ten, you should be completely relaxed.

■ Sometimes soothing music can enhance this process.

Exercise relieves stress by providing a positive outlet for the physical and emotional reactions that stress can cause.

Here are some examples of physical activities that can relieve stress:

- Jogging
- Dancing
- Riding a bike
- Swimming
- Doing exercises
- Playing a sport or game that requires physical effort

Emotional Support is comfort, reassurance, and encouragement from people who care about you. Having support from people who care about you can make you feel better when you are experiencing stress.

Communication is sharing your thoughts and feelings with other people. Communicating with others can help you to feel better. It can also help you to understand your problems and possibly help you to resolve them.

THANKS! TALKING TO YOU REALLY HELPS.

Because stress is a part of everyone's daily life, you need to make sure that you are prepared to deal with whatever stress comes along. This means staying healthy enough to handle stress.

Here are two ways that you can stay healthy so that you can be prepared to handle stress:

Eat healthy food. Avoid foods that contain too much
■ fat,
■ cholesterol,
■ sugar,
■ salt, and
■ caffeine.

Eat the right amounts of
■ fruit,
■ vegetables,
■ whole grains, and
■ beans, nuts, seeds, poultry, fish, and other sources of protein.

Also, drink enough water to keep your body functioning properly.

Get enough rest. You need at least eight hours of sleep every day.

You might not be able to control all of the stressors in your life, but you **can** control your reactions to them. How you react determines whether or not you will be harmed by a stressor.

In other words, the effect a stressor will have on your life depends on how **you** handle it.

Handle Stress
AFFIRMATIONS

- I feel better when I am calm.

- My body functions better when I am calm.

- My mind functions better when I am calm.

- I feel completely calm.

Handle Stress
AFFIRMATIONS

- I am breathing deeply.

- I am relaxing every part of my body.

- I am thinking positive thoughts.

- All tension is leaving my body.

Get Over It!

Handle Criticism & Rejection

You can handle criticism and rejection by learning about
- constructive criticism,
- destructive criticism,
- considering the source,
- dealing with people who are not qualified to criticize you,
- receiving constructive criticism,
- responding to constructive criticism,
- four steps for handling destructive criticism,
- feeling rejected,
- minimizing the effects of rejection, and
- overcoming rejection.

YOUR CLOTHES ARE **TOO BAGGY**, AND YOU NEED A HAIRCUT! **AND,** YOU ALSO NEED TO STAND UP STRAIGHTER, **AND...**

SHE'S WORSE THAN A JUDGE AT A DOG SHOW!

YOU'RE ALWAYS **CRiTiCiZiNG** ME, AND I DON'T LIKE IT!

WHAT DO YOU MEAN?

THAT'S EXACTLY WHAT I'VE FELT LIKE TELLING THE JUDGES AT THE DOG SHOWS!

Criticism is a judgmental evaluation of someone or something.

Criticism can be constructive or destructive.

Constructive criticism can have a positive effect on the person who is being criticized. The purpose of the constructive criticism is to help rather than to hurt others.

Constructive criticism usually reveals something that needs to be changed. When the person who has been criticized makes the necessary change, he or she can grow and become a better person.

For criticism to be constructive, it should be directed at things that can be changed and said in a kind and considerate way.

Destructive criticism usually has a negative effect on the person who is being criticized. The purpose of destructive criticism is often to hurt rather than to help others.

When nothing can be done to improve something, it is pointless to criticize it. Criticism directed at things that cannot be changed is usually destructive.

When someone criticizes you, it is important to "consider the source." This means evaluating the person to determine whether or not he or she is qualified to criticize you.

People who criticize you should be *intelligent and wise* enough to make judgments about you.

People who criticize you must be ***trustworthy.***
They must care about you and have your best
interests at heart.

THAT DRESS IS UNIQUE. YOU LOOK FABULOUS IN IT!

I THINK IT MAKES YOU LOOK **FAT!**

THE TRUTH IS, IT'S EXACTLY LIKE THE ONE I'M PLANNING TO WEAR. AND EVERYBODY WILL LAUGH IF WE COME DRESSED ALIKE.

People who criticize you must have *pure motives.* Their purpose in criticizing you should be to help you, not to hurt you.

People who criticize you must *be accurate.* They must have facts or other information to support what they say about you.

People should not be expressing their own *emotional problems* when they criticize you. People who are depressed, anxious, or upset might express their uncomfortable feelings by criticizing you. This kind of criticism has nothing to do with you and cannot help you in any way.

People should not be expressing their own *physical problems* when they criticize you. People who are hungry, tired, or sick might express their discomfort by criticizing you. This kind of criticism has nothing to do with you and cannot help you in any way.

I'VE BEEN THINKING ABOUT OUR RELATIONSHIP LATELY. YOU'RE JUST NO FUN ANYMORE!

DO YOU THINK THAT YOUR STAYING UP THREE NIGHTS IN A ROW TO STUDY MIGHT HAVE SOMETHING TO DO WITH YOUR SUDDEN CHANGE IN ATTITUDE TOWARD ME?

SHE LOOKS DOG TIRED!

People should not be *projecting their own faults* onto you when they criticize you. Sometimes people are unaware of having a certain fault that is unacceptable to them. At the same time, they accuse others of having the fault. This kind of criticism has nothing to do with you and cannot help you in any way.

To be qualified to criticize you, people must
- be intelligent and wise,
- be trustworthy,
- have pure motives, and
- be accurate.

To be qualified to criticize you, people must **not** use criticism to
- express their own emotional problems,
- express their own physical problems, or
- project their faults onto you.

Sometimes when you consider the source, you will determine that the person who is criticizing you is **not** qualified to do so. When this happens, ask the person to stop criticizing you.

Sometimes someone who is not qualified to criticize you will continue to do so even after you have asked him or her to stop. When this happens, try to ignore what is being said or separate yourself from the person.

Most people are more open to receiving constructive criticism when
- they are feeling well emotionally and physically,
- they are not preoccupied, and
- they receive it in private.

Sometimes someone might want to share some constructive criticism with you when you are not feeling well physically or emotionally. Your mind most likely will be on your problems and not on what is being said. If this happens, explain how you feel and ask the person to share the criticism with you when you are feeling better.

Sometimes someone might want to share some constructive criticism with you when you are busy doing something else. Your attention most likely will be focused on what you are doing and not on what is being said. If this happens, explain that you are preoccupied and ask the person to wait and share the criticism with you when you can give your full attention.

Sometimes someone might want to share some constructive criticism with you in front of other people. This could become embarrassing for everyone. If this happens, ask the person to wait until the criticism can be shared privately.

To benefit from constructive criticism, you need to respond to it appropriately. To do this, follow these six steps:

Step 1: Listen carefully while you are being criticized.

Try to avoid interrupting when someone is criticizing you. Instead of defending yourself or making excuses for whatever is being criticized, focus on what is being said.

I DON'T WANT TO HURT YOUR FEELINGS, BUT YOU EAT WAY TOO MUCH JUNK FOOD, AND YOU'RE GAINING A LOT OF WEIGHT!

Step 2: Thank the person who has criticized you.

Since constructive criticism can be beneficial, it is important to make people feel comfortable about sharing it with you. If you make people feel uncomfortable about offering constructive criticism, they might stop doing it. This could cause you to miss out on some wonderful opportunities to grow and to become a better person.

Step 3: Carefully consider the criticism you have received.

Try to determine whether or not the criticism is *valid.* Consider whether or not it is true and is about something that can be corrected. Keep an open mind and examine the information that has been presented. It might help to talk to several other qualified people and get their opinions about the criticism.

Step 4: Decide what you need to do about the criticism.

If you determine that the criticism is not valid, you will **not** need to make any change. However, if you determine that the criticism is valid, you will need to decide exactly what change needs to be made.

Step 5: Follow through with whatever you have decided to do.

Make whatever change is necessary.

Step 6: Talk to the person who criticized you.

If you decided to make a change, the person who criticized you most likely will appreciate knowing about it.

If you decided against making a change, it would be good to let the person know. Then he or she will not feel ignored and won't continue criticizing you.

Just as constructive criticism can be helpful, destructive criticism can be harmful.

Destructive criticism can damage your self-esteem and confidence.

This can cause you to become less productive and keep you from achieving your full potential. To avoid the negative effects of destructive criticism, you need to handle it appropriately. To do this, follow these four steps:

Step 1: Let the person who is criticizing you know that his or her destructive criticism is unacceptable.

Look the person in the eye, and explain that you feel his or her criticism is not valid. Then, tell the person why you think this is true.

Step 2: Tell the person who is criticizing you how the criticism makes you feel.

Let the person know if the criticism has hurt or upset you.

Step 3: Stop listening to the criticism.

Finally, ask the person who is criticizing you to stop. If he or she will not stop, ignore the criticism or separate yourself from the person.

Step 4: Put the criticism aside.

Avoid thinking about the criticism. Replace it with positive thoughts about yourself.

It will help if you spend time with people who genuinely like you and who will help you identify and affirm your positive qualities.

Sometimes being criticized can cause you to feel rejected. Feeling rejected means feeling unloved or unwanted.

THERE'S CHERYL! LET'S PRETEND WE DON'T SEE HER SO SHE WON'T ASK TO HANG AROUND WITH US!

Feeling rejected can have a negative effect on you. It can cause you to feel inferior. It can lower your self-confidence and affect your ability to achieve. This can make you feel unhappy.

You can minimize the negative effects of feeling rejected by realizing these things:

Every human being is valuable and deserves to be accepted by others.

WHAT DO YOU **MEAN?** EVERYONE IS GOOD AT **SOMETHING!**

EVERYONE EXCEPT ME...

Even though human beings are valuable, they are not perfect.

Everyone has ways in which he or she can improve. Everyone misbehaves and has problems at one time or another.

I MADE A **FOOL** OF MYSELF WHEN I TRIED OUT FOR CHEERLEADER LAST YEAR!

THAT'S ONLY BECAUSE YOU DIDN'T WORK HARD ENOUGH ON YOUR ROUTINE. BUT YOU CAN DO BETTER THIS YEAR!

Healthy, intelligent people believe in the value of every human being. At the same time, they realize that human beings are not perfect.

Sometimes healthy, intelligent people reject misbehavior or problems in other people. However, they do not reject the people themselves.

JUST BECAUSE YOU FAILED **ONCE** DOESN'T MEAN YOU'RE A FAILURE! EVERYONE FAILS ONCE IN A WHILE...

People who reject others rather than their misbehavior are not acting intelligently or responsibly.

Therefore, you must not think that something is wrong with you if someone rejects you. Instead, you need to realize that something is wrong with the attitude of the person who is rejecting you.

Sometimes you can persuade people to stop rejecting you.

If a person's rejection of you is based on inaccurate information, it might help to talk with the person. This can give you a chance to correct any misconceptions and might alter how the person feels toward you.

If a person's rejection is based on valid criticism of you, it might help to make some necessary changes. Doing this might alter how the person feels toward you.

OH, I'M SORRY! I DIDN'T REALIZE WE WERE BEING **RUDE** TO YOU.

HONEST! I DIDN'T SEE WHO SHOVED YOU IN THE LOCKER!

THE TRUTH IS, YOU'RE NOT IN OUR GROUP BECAUSE YOU'RE NOT POPULAR ENOUGH!

Sometimes, no matter what you say or do, you cannot make a person stop rejecting you.

When this happens, you need to do several things:

■ Remember that you are a human being and, even though you are not perfect, you are still valuable.

▪ Remember, it is the person who rejects you—not you—who has the problems.

■ Avoid being around any person who rejects you.

LET'S GO SOMEPLACE WHERE WE DON'T HAVE TO BE AROUND THEM.

NOW YOU'RE TALKING!

■ Spend time with people who like and appreciate you.

You can benefit from learning to recognize whether criticism is constructive or destructive.

I THINK YOU FORGOT YOUR ROUTINE DURING CHEERLEADING TRYOUTS BECAUSE IT WAS TOO COMPLICATED.

DO YOU REALLY THINK SO?

You can also benefit from learning to recognize whether or not a person is qualified to criticize you.

I CAN SHOW YOU A ROUTINE THAT'S SIMPLE BUT VERY **FLASHY!**

LET HER SHOW YOU, CHERYL. SHE'S TAKEN DANCE FOR YEARS AND COULD TEACH YOU SOME GREAT THINGS.

SOUNDS GOOD TO ME!

Remember, if someone who is qualified criticizes you and you receive the criticism appropriately, you can grow and become a better person.

Handle Criticism & Rejection
AFFIRMATIONS

- I gratefully receive constructive criticism.

- Constructive criticism helps me determine how I can improve my life.

- I make all necessary improvements.

- The improvements I make cause me to become a better person.

Handle Criticism & Rejection
AFFIRMATIONS

- Like all human beings, I am valuable.

- I deserve to be accepted.

- I avoid people who reject me.

- I spend time with people who like and appreciate me.

Get Over It!

Handle Rude People

You can get along with rude people by
- understanding why getting along with some people can be difficult,
- understanding why some people are rude,
- knowing why you need to learn how to deal with rude people,
- following eight steps to getting along, and
- remembering three wise sayings.

The majority of people are kind and helpful. Therefore, getting along with most people is easy.

However, some people are not kind and helpful. Getting along with these people can be difficult.

There are several reasons why getting along with some people can be difficult.

Some people are difficult to get along with because they are **self-centered.**

People who are self-centered do not care about others as much as they care about themselves. They can be greedy, selfish, and unfair. Self-centered people usually take more from other people than they give to them.

Some people are difficult to get along with because they have a **superior attitude.**

People with superior attitudes think that they are better than other people. They act as though they know more and can do more than others. People with superior attitudes often try to make the people around them feel inferior.

Some people are difficult to get along with because they are **bossy.**

People who are bossy try to control others. They tell people around them what to do and expect them to do as they're told. Bossy people are bad sports when things do not happen the way that they want them to happen.

Some people are difficult to get along with because they **bully** others.

People who are bullies like to frighten or hurt others who are smaller or weaker than they are. They try to solve their problems by threatening or fighting with others.

Some people are difficult to get along with because they are **offensive.**

People who are offensive do not care about the thoughts and feelings of other people. They do things that hurt or insult others. Offensive people often cause those around them to be uncomfortable.

Some people are difficult to get along with because they are **negative.**

People who are negative are never satisfied. They whine and complain about everyone and everything. Negative people say things and do things that make themselves and the people around them unhappy.

Some people are difficult to get along with because they are **irresponsible.**

People who are irresponsible do not do what they are supposed to do. They often fail to keep their commitments. Irresponsible people disappoint the people who depend on them.

Some people are difficult to get along with because they are **stubborn.**

People who are stubborn have a hard time compromising or giving in to others. They have difficulty admitting that they are wrong or saying that they are sorry. Stubborn people often cause other people to feel frustrated.

Some people are difficult to get along with because they are **unresponsive.**

People who are unresponsive act as though they are not interested in others. They do not do their part to keep a conversation going. They have a hard time sharing feelings with others. Communicating with unresponsive people is not easy.

Some people are difficult to get along with because they are **insincere.**

People who are insincere are phony. They pretend to be someone other than who they are. Their actions and words do not show how they truly think and feel. It is hard to trust insincere people.

Rude people feel and act the way they do for several reasons.

Some people are rude because they are ignorant.

They have not learned acceptable behavior. They do not know the correct way to act.

Some people are rude because they have personal problems.

They have problems in their lives that are not being solved. They act the way that they do because their problems cause them to be frustrated and upset.

Some people are rude because they feel inferior.

They do not feel that they are as good as other people. They act the way that they do to try to prove that they are as good as, or better than, others.

Some people are rude because they need attention.

They need to have people notice them. They act the way that they do so that others will pay attention to them.

Some people are rude because they are afraid.

They are afraid that other people might hurt them in some way. They act the way that they do so that people will fear them and not bother them.

I DON'T WANT THOSE GUYS TO MESS AROUND WITH ME AND HURT ME. I'VE GOT TO SHOW THEM I'M TOUGH!

Some people are rude because they are angry.

They are angry about something that has upset them. They express their anger by being unkind.

Learning how to get along with rude people is necessary because you are likely to come in contact with rude people often.

Some of the rude people that you encounter are people you know. You might be around these people often.

No matter how often you are around a rude person, he or she can upset you.

HE COULD SIT **ANYWHERE!** WHY DOES HE HAVE TO SIT NEXT TO ME? HE IRRITATES ME SO MUCH I CAN'T CONCENTRATE!

OHHH... IS DE WIDDOW DWEEB DOING HER WIDDOW WESSON?

Rude people can make your life unpleasant if you don't know how to deal with them.

If you do not want rude people to make your life unpleasant, you need to respond to them in a positive way. Here are eight steps to help you do this:

Step 1: Try to understand rude people.

Try to understand **why** rude people act the way that they do. Try to find out whether they
■ are ignorant,
■ have personal problems,
■ feel inferior,
■ need attention,
■ are afraid, or
■ are angry.

Do these things to learn about a rude person whom you encounter frequently:

- Put yourself in the other person's place. Try to imagine how you would think and act if you were that person.
- Talk directly to the person.
- Talk to people who know the person well.

Step 2: Accept rude people the way they are.

Do not try to change other people. Realize that changing someone else is impossible. People can only change themselves.

WELL, IT'S A SAFE BET BRAD WILL NEVER CHANGE!

MOVE IT SCUM BAG!

UMPH!

You can accept someone who is rude more easily if you remember that every person has good qualities. Discover and concentrate on the good qualities about a person rather than on his or her faults.

HE REALLY TRIES HARD WHEN HE WANTS TO. HE WAS REALLY HELPFUL WHEN WE WORKED ON THAT GROUP PROJECT TOGETHER...

TAP TAP TAP

Step 3: Forgive rude people.

Hate and anger are powerful emotions. They can cause you to be upset and can make you very unhappy. When you hate other people or stay angry at them, you are hurting yourself.

When you forgive someone, the hate or anger you feel for the person often goes away. You usually feel better and so does the person you forgive. Understanding someone who is rude and accepting that person makes it easier for you to forgive him or her.

Step 4: Be kind to rude people.

Do whatever you can to assure people that you do not want to hurt them in any way. If you are kind and supportive, people most likely will feel comfortable around you and will not need to act in a negative way.

Do whatever you can to make people feel good about themselves. Compliment them. Encourage them so that they will not need to get attention in negative ways.

Step 5: Talk to rude people about their behavior.

Tell them in a kind way just how you feel about their misbehavior. Tell them about how it affects you. Ask them to stop doing what they are doing.

When you talk to a rude person about his or her misbehavior, try to do these things:

■ Talk to the person when you are calm so that you do not say things that you might regret.
■ Talk to the person when he or she is not upset.
■ Talk to the person when he or she has time to listen to you.
■ Talk to the person face to face, and look into his or her eyes when you talk.

Step 6: Do not take rude people's behavior personally.

Do not assume something is wrong with you when someone treats you badly. Remember, a rude person's misbehavior is his or her problem, not yours.

I DON'T KNOW... SOMETIMES I JUST CAN'T HELP MYSELF.

Following these six steps will probably help you feel better. Also, if you respond in a positive way to someone who is rude, he or she may stop misbehaving. However, if a rude person does not change, you need to follow two additional steps.

Step 7: Do not pay attention to rude people when they are misbehaving.

Try to ignore rude people when they treat you badly. Do not react to their misbehavior.

It is harder for someone to upset you or to make your life unpleasant if you ignore the person.

HUH?

AH, YES! THE OL' SILENT TREATMENT. GETS THEM EVERY TIME.

Step 8: Avoid being around rude people.

As much as possible, stay away from people who treat you badly. This makes it harder for them to bother you.

It might be hard to avoid being around a rude person whom you must see often, such as a teacher, coach, or relative. To avoid such a person, you might need to ask an adult whom you trust to help you.

Tell the adult exactly how you feel about the rude person. Ask for help in deciding whether or not you should avoid the rude person. If you agree that the person should be avoided, ask the adult for advice on how you can avoid being around the person.

Here are three wise sayings that can help you learn to get along with rude people:

Saying #1: A soft word turns away wrath.

Speaking kindly to an angry person might help him or her to calm down. You might be able to help the person overcome the anger that is making him or her a rude person. In this way, you are doing a favor for everyone.

Saying #2: You can't fight fire with fire.

You cannot put out a fire with fire. A fire must be put out with something else, such as water. It is the same with negative behavior. You cannot stop a person from being unkind by being unkind yourself. You cannot stop an argument by arguing.

To stop negative behavior, you must respond in a positive way.

Saying #3: Be kind to your enemies, and you won't have any.

It is hard to be unkind to someone who is being kind to you. It is hard to hate someone who is caring toward you. When you are kind and caring to someone, you make it hard for that person to hate and mistreat you. Instead, the person is encouraged to like you and to treat you well.

Sometimes you might find it difficult to be kind to a person who is cruel to you. However, it is not impossible. In most cases, kindness usually is the only thing that works with a rude person. Being cruel to someone who is being cruel only makes the person want to become more cruel. Kindness is powerful and has the potential to overcome cruelty.

Rude people are a part of everyone's life. You can get along with these people if you learn how to respond to them in a positive way.

Handle Rude People
AFFIRMATIONS

- I seek to understand difficult people rather than react to them.

- My understanding helps me forgive people when they misbehave.

- I overcome the misbehavior of others by being kind.

- My kindness is motivated by my respect for all human beings.

Handle Rude People
AFFIRMATIONS

- I put my energy into getting along with difficult people rather than getting revenge.

- The purpose of my communications is to help rather than hurt others.

- The purpose of my actions is to create positive rather than negative results.

- I do not allow the misbehavior of difficult people to have a negative effect on my life.

Get Over It!

Handle Tough Situations

You can handle tough situations if you know
- what tough situations are,
- the different types of tough situations,
- the various origins of tough situations,
- the six steps for handling tough situations that you create,
- the six steps for handling tough situations that you did not create, and
- the things that make it easier to handle tough situations.

A tough situation is one that jeopardizes someone's happiness or well-being.

MY PARENTS GROUNDED ME BECAUSE I LIED TO THEM. NOW I CAN'T GO TO BASEBALL PRACTICE FOR A WEEK.

BUT THAT MEANS THAT YOU WON'T BE ABLE TO PITCH IN SATURDAY'S GAME!

A tough situation can hurt you or someone else.

Some tough situations can cause **physical harm**.

THE WORST SITUATION I EVER FACED WAS THE TIME I WENT HIKING WITH SOME FRIENDS. WE WERE LOST FOR OVER 24 HOURS. THE TEMPERATURE DROPPED AND WE NEARLY FROZE TO DEATH!

Some tough situations can cause **mental or emotional harm**.

THE MOST DIFFICULT SITUATION I EVER FACED WAS MY PARENTS' DIVORCE. MY DAD WANTED ME TO LIVE WITH **HIM** AND MY MOM WANTED ME TO LIVE WITH **HER.** I KNEW NO MATTER WHERE I LIVED, SOMEONE'S FEELINGS WOULD BE HURT!

Short-term tough situations last for a short period of time such as an hour or a day.

ONE OF THE WORST SITUATIONS I EVER FACED, HAPPENED AT A PARK. THE CHILD I WAS BABYSITTING WANDERED AWAY WHILE I WAS TAKING HIS SISTER TO THE RESTROOM. LUCKILY, A POLICE OFFICER FOUND THE CHILD AND BROUGHT HIM BACK TO ME.

Long-term tough situations last for a long period of time such as several days, weeks, or months.

THE PROBLEM WITH MY DIFFICULT SITUATION IS THAT IT'S GOING TO LAST A LONG TIME. IF I MISS PRACTICE FOR A WEEK, I'LL PROBABLY GET KICKED OFF THE TEAM AND WON'T BE ABLE TO PLAY BASE-BALL FOR THE REST OF THE YEAR!

UGH!

Whether a tough situation is short-term or long-term, it seldom disappears automatically.

In fact, a tough situation that is not handled appropriately can become worse and possibly can create additional tough situations.

To handle a tough situation appropriately, it is important to determine who or what created it.

Sometimes **you** create a tough situation by breaking a natural law.

A **natural law** is a specific principle established by nature.

When you break a natural law, you often experience the negative consequences that automatically occur when the law is broken.

This puts you in a tough situation.

Sometimes *you* create a tough situation by breaking a man-made law.

A **man-made law** is a rule established by people.

When you break a man-made law, you often are forced to pay a penalty that is imposed on you by the people who enforce the law.

This puts you in a tough situation.

Common sense is good judgement that is based on simple logic and reasoning.

Sometimes you create a tough situation by disregarding your common sense and acting against it.

I PROBABLY SHOULDN'T GET IN A STRANGER'S CAR...BUT...OH WELL, I WOULDN'T HAVE TO GO VERY FAR WITH HIM...I'M JUST A FEW BLOCKS FROM HOME...

WANT A RIDE HOME?

LISTEN TO ME KID! YOU'RE BARKING UP THE WRONG TREE!

When you act against your common sense, you often experience the negative consequences that automatically occur when you do something that is illogical and senseless.

JESSICA JONES HAS BEEN MISSING FOR TWO DAYS. SHE WAS LAST SEEN WALKING HOME FROM SCHOOL ON...

Natural circumstances beyond your control are occurrences, caused by nature, that you cannot prevent or change.

Sometimes natural circumstances beyond your control create tough situations.

Human circumstances beyond your control are occurrences, caused by other people, that you cannot prevent or change.

Sometimes human circumstances beyond your control can create tough situations.

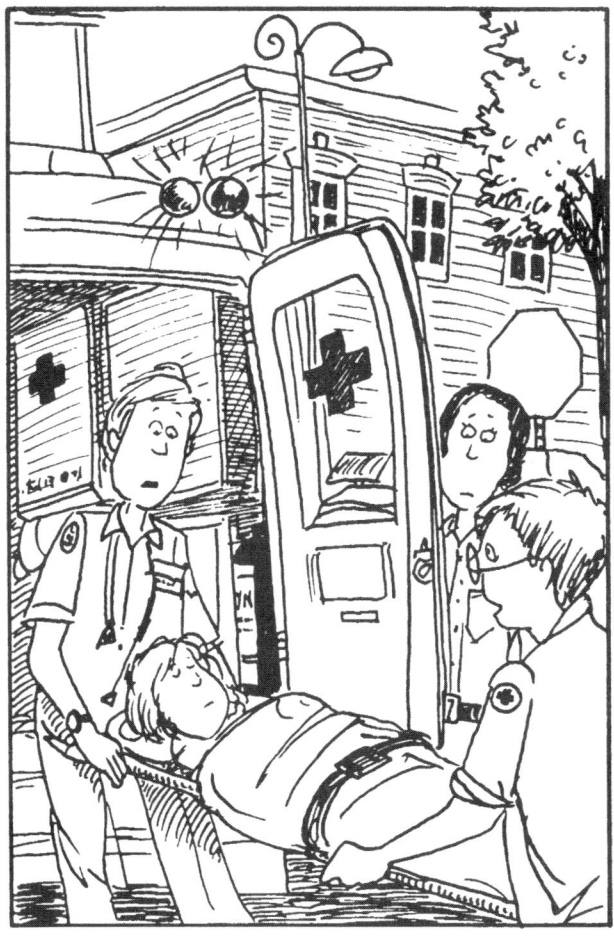

Here are six steps for handling tough situations that *you* create:

Step 1: Face it.

Admit that you are experiencing a tough situation. Do not pretend that everything is OK.

Step 2: Accept it.

Accept this fact: The tough situation is not going to go away automatically. Realize that you are going to have to put time and effort into resolving it.

Step 3: Think about it.

Find out the answers to these questions:

■ What did I do to create this situation?
■ What consequences will I have to experience?

I LOST AMY'S JACKET, SO I'M GOING TO HAVE TO FACE HER AND ADMIT WHAT I'VE DONE. SHE'LL PROBABLY BE PRETTY MAD AT ME, BUT I'M JUST GOING TO HAVE TO TAKE IT.

Step 4: Decide what to do.

Find out the answers to these questions:

- What do I need to do to make the people I may have hurt feel better?
- What do I need to do to make myself feel better?

Make sure that the things you decide to do are not harmful to yourself or to others.

Step 5: Do what you have decided to do.

If you have hurt other people, you need to do what you can to make them feel better. Make sure that you
■ admit that you have done something wrong,
■ say that you are sorry,
■ do whatever you can to make up for your wrongdoing (make sure that your efforts are acceptable to the people you have hurt), and
■ try not to do the same thing again.

You also need to make yourself feel better. Make sure that you

- remember that you are a human being (you are not perfect, and it is normal for you to make mistakes),
- forgive yourself when you do something that is wrong,
- learn whatever you can from the situation, and
- try not to do the same thing again.

I FEEL BAD ABOUT LOSING AMY'S JACKET, BUT THERE'S NOTHING MORE I CAN DO ABOUT IT NOW. I'VE JUST GOT TO FORGIVE MYSELF AND GO ON. ONE THING'S FOR SURE, I'M NOT EVER GOING TO BORROW ANYTHING THAT EXPENSIVE AGAIN.

Step 6: Talk about your thoughts and feelings.

A tough situation can cause you to have many thoughts and feelings that should not be ignored. Pay attention to them. Share them with someone else. When you talk to someone, you need to make sure that the person is

■ someone who you respect and can trust,

■ someone who cares about you, and

■ someone who is old enough and wise enough to help you.

MOM, I CAN'T BELIEVE THAT AMY IS STILL MAD AT ME ABOUT HER JACKET.

Talking about a tough situation one time will probably not make everything OK. Therefore, you need to continue to talk about your thoughts and feelings for as long as you feel a need to do so.

I FEEL AS BAD AS AMY ABOUT THE LOSS...NOT ONLY WAS IT EMBARRASSING FOR ME, I DIDN'T GET THE BIKE I'VE BEEN SAVING FOR SIX MONTHS TO BUY.

Here are six steps for handling tough situations that you did **not** create:

Step 1: Face it.

Admit that you are experiencing a tough situation. Do not pretend that everything is OK.

Step 2: Accept it.

Accept this fact: The tough situation is not going to go away automatically. Realize that you are going to have to put some time and effort into resolving it.

Step 3: Think about it.

Find out the answers to these questions:

- What happened to create this tough situation?
- What is going to happen to me?

LET'S SEE...IT'S ALL BEN'S IDEA FOR ME TO WRITE HIS TERM PAPER, AND IF I DON'T DO IT, HE'LL PROBABLY GET MAD. HE MIGHT EVEN STOP BEING MY FRIEND.

Step 4: Decide what to do.

Find out the answers to these questions:

- What can I do to make the situation better?
- What can I do to make myself feel better?
- What can I do to make the other people who are involved in this situation feel better?

Step 5: Do what you have decided to do.

If possible, you should
- talk to the people who created the tough situation (if you cannot talk to them, talk to someone else),
- try to understand why these people did what they did,
- try to forgive them,
- do not blame yourself in any way, and
- do whatever you can to make yourself and the other people involved in the situation feel better.

I REALIZE THAT HISTORY IS A TOUGH SUBJECT FOR YOU, SO I CAN UNDERSTAND WHY YOU WOULD WANT ME TO WRITE YOUR TERM PAPER. BUT WHAT YOU'RE ASKING ME TO DO ISN'T FAIR! IT WOULD TAKE A LOT OF WORK, AND IT MIGHT GET ME IN TROUBLE. SO WHAT I PROPOSE IS THAT I TELL YOU STEP-BY-STEP HOW TO WRITE A PAPER AND THEN YOU DO IT YOURSELF...

Step 6: Talk about your thoughts and feelings.

It is important that you continue to talk over your thoughts and feelings about the tough situation until you feel better.

IT STILL UPSETS ME TO THINK THAT BEN EXPECTED **ME** TO WRITE HIS TERM PAPER...

It will be easier to handle a tough situation if you are calm.

A good way to calm yourself is to
■ stop whatever you are doing,
■ take several deep breaths and let them out slowly, and
■ relax your body.

Here is one way to relax your body:

■ Slowly count to ten.
■ Tense your entire body more and more with each count. By the time you reach 10, your body should feel completely tense from your head to your toes.
■ Slowly count backwards from ten.
■ Relax your entire body more and more with each count. By the time you reach 10, your body should feel completely relaxed all over.

It will be easier to handle a tough situation if you slow down your thoughts and focus them on dealing with the situation.

NOW LET ME JUST THINK FOR A MINUTE...WHERE DID I **LAST** USE MY PURSE?

Avoid doing anything that will cloud your thinking.

This includes using substances such as alcohol or non-prescription drugs to calm yourself.

It will be easier to handle a tough situation if you remember these six facts:

Fact #1. There are some good things about every situation. Try not to focus on the bad things about a situation. Instead, look for the good things and focus your attention on them. This will help prevent you from becoming so depressed that you cannot deal appropriately with the situation.

Fact #2. Things could always be worse. Try to realize that no matter how bad a situation seems to be, it could always be worse. Be thankful that it is not worse. Being thankful will help you to feel better.

Fact #3. Every problem has a solution. When a tough situation creates problems for you, try not to waste your time and energy feeling bad about them. Instead, realize that there are solutions to your problems. Spend your time and energy finding the solutions. This will help you to overcome the problems and to feel better.

Fact #4. Every person can find the solutions to his or her problems. Remember that every person has the ability on their own or with the help of others, to find the solutions to any problem. Realizing this will help prevent you from giving up before your problems are resolved.

BECAUSE I'M GROUNDED, I HAVE TO MISS PRACTICE FOR A WEEK. IS THERE ANY WAY I CAN MAKE UP FOR THE TIME I'LL MISS SO I WON'T GET KICKED OFF THE TEAM?

I THINK WE CAN WORK OUT SOMETHING

Fact #5. "This too shall pass." Remember that just as every experience has a beginning, it also has an ending. This includes any tough situation that you encounter. Realizing this can make it easier for you to endure difficult times.

Fact #6. "Time heals all wounds." Remember, by handling tough situations in a positive way, the pain you experience most likely will fade with the passing of time. Realizing this can make it easier for you to endure difficult times.

IT'S GOING TO TAKE TIME FOR MOM AND DAD TO GET OVER MY LYING TO THEM. IT'S ALSO GOING TO TAKE TIME FOR ME TO REBUILD THEIR TRUST IN ME. I GUESS I'LL JUST HAVE TO BE PATIENT FOR A WHILE...

Tough situations do not have negative endings automatically.

Tough situations can have positive endings if they are handled appropriately.

STRIKE THREE! YOU'RE OUT!

Tough situations that are handled appropriately can help you to grow and to become a better person.

WE'RE **PROUD** OF YOU, BEN!

Handle Tough Situations
AFFIRMATIONS

- Every problem has a solution.

- I am able to find solutions to my problems.

- I do whatever is necessary to solve my problems.

- Every time I solve a problem, I grow and become a better person.

Handle Tough Situations
AFFIRMATIONS

- I gain something from every experience.

- I learn valuable lessons from difficult experiences.

- Difficult experiences help me become more tolerant and understanding of others.

- Surviving a difficult experience helps me realize that I can survive, and I become less fearful.

Get Over It!

Get Rid of Bad Habits

You can get rid of your bad habits if you
■ understand what habits are,
■ learn the differences between good and
  bad habits,
■ recognize your bad habits,
■ know why you develop bad habits,
■ follow the six steps for eliminating bad
  habits, and
■ remember some things that make it easier to
  overcome bad habits.

YOU SHOULDN'T BITE YOUR NAILS. THAT'S A **BAD HABIT.**

I ALWAYS BITE MY NAILS WHEN I'M NERVOUS, AND I'M NERVOUS ABOUT THE TEST TODAY.

THAT TEST IS NO BIG DEAL. I'LL WAIT UNTIL THE LAST MINUTE TO STUDY.

YEAH, AND THAT'S A BAD HABIT OF YOURS!

A habit is something that you have done so often or for so long that you do it without thinking.

YEAH, I GUESS YOU'RE RIGHT! I ALWAYS WAIT UNTIL THE LAST MINUTE— FOR AS LONG AS I CAN REMEMBER.

I KNOW. I'VE BEEN BITING MY NAILS SINCE I WAS SIX.

If you are like most people, you have many habits.

Some of your habits are good. Your **good habits** can benefit you and possibly the people around you.

Your good habits also can benefit the world in which you live.

Some of your habits might be bad. Your **bad habits** can annoy or harm you or the people around you.

Your bad habits also can be harmful to the world in which you live.

COUGH GAG

There are at least four ways to tell whether or not you have a bad habit.

#1: You might have a bad habit if you cannot keep yourself from doing something that you don't want to do or should not do.

I WISH I COULD STOP BITING MY NAILS!

BITING A RAWHIDE BONE IS SO MUCH MORE SATISFYING!

#2: You might have a bad habit if you continually do something that is unpleasant and bothers other people.

WELL, IF YOU WANT **MY** OPINION...

THAT'S A BAD HABIT OF YOURS!

PAM, YOU INTERRUPTED AGAIN!

#3: You might have a bad habit if you continually lie about something that you do so that no one will know that you do it.

#4: You might have a bad habit if you constantly do something that makes you feel guilty.

There are many reasons why you might have a bad habit.

Ignorance might be a reason why you develop a bad habit. You might do something that is unacceptable because you do not know that you should not do it.

Peer pressure might be a reason why you develop a bad habit. You might do something that is unacceptable because one of your peers is doing it.

AREN'T YOU GOING TO BUCKLE YOUR SAFETY BELT?

NAH! NO ONE IN MY FAMILY WEARS ONE. IT'S TOO CONFINING!

Carelessness might be a reason why you develop a bad habit. You might do something that is unacceptable because you do not care whether or not you do what is right.

Reacting to a problem might be a reason why you develop a bad habit. You might try to get rid of a problem by doing something that is unacceptable.

WHY DO YOU ALWAYS SHAKE YOUR FOOT LIKE THAT?

IT'S JUST A BAD HABIT. I DO IT WHEN I'M NERVOUS...AND WITH A REPORT CARD LIKE MINE, I'M REALLY NERVOUS!

Anxiety might be a reason why you develop a bad habit. You might do something that is unacceptable to relieve the nervous energy that comes from worrying about something.

Boredom might be a reason why you develop a bad habit. You might do something that is unacceptable because you do not have anything else to do.

YOU'RE DEVELOPING A BAD HABIT OF WATCHING T.V. **ALL** OF THE TIME!

THERE'S NOTHING ELSE TO DO! I'M BORED.

Feeling inferior might be a reason why you develop a bad habit. You might feel unimportant and do something that is unacceptable so that people will pay attention to you.

Feeling overwhelmed might be a reason why you develop a bad habit. You might think that you cannot handle the problems in your life, and you might react by doing something that is unacceptable.

MOM AND DAD WILL FREAK OUT IF THEY CATCH ME. BUT IF I DON'T GET OUT OF HERE, I'LL *GO CRAZY!*

No matter why you have a bad habit, you will be happier if you get rid of it. You can get rid of a bad habit by following these six steps:

Step 1: Admit that you have a bad habit.

Admit it to yourself.

It might also help to admit your bad habit to someone you trust.

I'VE GOT A TERRIBLE HABIT OF ALWAYS BITING MY NAILS.

Step 2: Realize that you need to quit.

Ask yourself these two questions:

■ Why is this habit bad?
■ How will I benefit if I get rid of this habit?

List your answers to these questions on a sheet of paper.

Ask some other people the same two questions:

▪ Why do you think that this habit is bad?
▪ How do you think that I will benefit if I get rid of this habit?

Again, list the answers you receive on a sheet of paper.

Step 3: Encourage yourself to quit.

Put the two lists containing the answers to your questions in a place where you will see them often.

Read both lists to yourself at the beginning of each day. Read them again at the end of the day.

IT'S **GROSS,** IT'S **UGLY,** IT'S...

THAT LIST IS ENOUGH TO MAKE ANYBODY STOP BITING THEIR NAILS.

Step 4: Prepare yourself to quit.

Talk to one or more people. They can be family members or friends. Tell these people that you would like to quit your bad habit. Ask them to remind you to stop if they see you start again.

Do other things to remind yourself to quit. Here are a few suggestions:

- Write notes to yourself, and put them in places where you will be sure to see them.
- Tie a string or put a Band-Aid around your finger.
- Put a sticker or small piece of tape on your clothing or the back of your hand.
- Put a mark or write a message to yourself with a non-permanent ink pen on the back of your hand.

Step 5: Quit one day at a time.

It is not a good idea to promise yourself that you are going to quit your bad habit **forever**. This promise can seem like an impossible goal. It can discourage you and cause you to give up before you have succeeded.

Quitting one day at a time is a better goal because it is one that you can achieve.

Here is how to quit one day at a time:

■ Begin each day by promising yourself that you will not give in to your bad habit for **that day**.

■ With the help of your lists, other people, and your personal reminders, quit for **that day**.

■ At the end of the day, think about your success and share it with another person.

The good feeling that you get from succeeding will make you want to try again the next day. If you can succeed for 21 consecutive days, your bad habit most likely will be broken.

Step 6: Replace the bad habit with a good habit.

When you finally get rid of your bad habit, you most likely will feel as though you have lost something. This may cause you to feel uncomfortable.

To avoid this "sense of loss," you need to replace the bad habit with a good habit.

It will be easier for you to get rid of a bad habit if you do these things:

Keep yourself busy so that you will not have time to think about or to continue your bad habit.

Spend time with people who will encourage you. Encouragement from other people can motivate you to continue your efforts toward succeeding.

Keep track of your success by

■ making a chart and putting a sticker on it for every day that you succeed or

■ marking off your successful days on a calendar.

Reward yourself whenever you succeed. Do something that you like to do, or allow yourself to have something that you want at the end of a successful day. Make sure that your rewards are things that are good for you.

HEY, THIS IS FUN!

TOMORROW I'M GETTING MORE COLORS.

It will be easier for you to get rid of a bad habit if you avoid doing certain things.

Do not allow yourself to think, "I can't!" Instead, think positive thoughts, such as:

■ "I can do anything that I want to do!"

■ "I can control this bad habit instead of letting it control me."

Do not allow yourself to focus on your failures. If you are not successful for a period of time, don't dwell on it. Instead, concentrate on your past successes. Also, think about succeeding in the future.

Do not allow yourself to focus on any pleasure that you might get from your bad habit. Instead, concentrate on the benefits that you will gain from getting rid of the bad habit.

Do not allow yourself to make excuses for your bad habit. Inventing excuses makes it easier for you to fail. Here are some common excuses that you should avoid telling yourself:

- "No one is perfect."
- "Everyone has at least one bad habit."
- "My friend has a habit that is worse than mine."
- "It's just a little habit that doesn't really matter."
- "I don't have time to quit."
- "I'm not ready to quit today. I'll quit some other day."

It takes effort to get rid of a bad habit. It is seldom easy.

OH, NO YOU DON'T! IT'S NOT EASY TO GIVE UP A BAD HABIT. YOU'VE GOT TO BE WILLING TO **WORK** AT IT!

GULP!

If you do not develop a bad habit, you will not have to go through the effort of overcoming it. This is why you should not do anything that might become a bad habit. Talk to the people you know. Observe them. Find out what their bad habits are. Then, avoid developing the same bad habits.

A good rule to follow is this:

Do not become involved with anything that is harmful to

■ you,

■ other people, or

■ your environment.

If you have tried your best but cannot give up a bad habit, it may be for one or two reasons.

1. Your bad habit might be an **addiction**. You might have become dependent on that habit, and you might be afraid that you will not be OK if you give it up.

2. You might have **problems** that have not been resolved. These problems might be the reason for your bad habit.

MAYBE I EAT TOO MUCH JUNK FOOD BECAUSE I HAVE A PROBLEM MEETING GIRLS!

HMMM...

In either case, you most likely will need professional help with

▪ overcoming your addiction or
▪ solving your problems.

Getting rid of a bad habit can make you a better person, and it can enhance your life.

Therefore, the work that you put into getting rid of a bad habit will be worth it in the long run.

Get Rid of Bad Habits
AFFIRMATIONS

- There is only one of me in the whole world.

- I am valuable.

- I take care of myself.

- I do only those things that are good for me.

Get Rid of Bad Habits
AFFIRMATIONS

- Bad habits are not good for me.

- I do only those things that are good for me.

- There is no room in my life for bad habits.

- I replace bad habits with good habits.